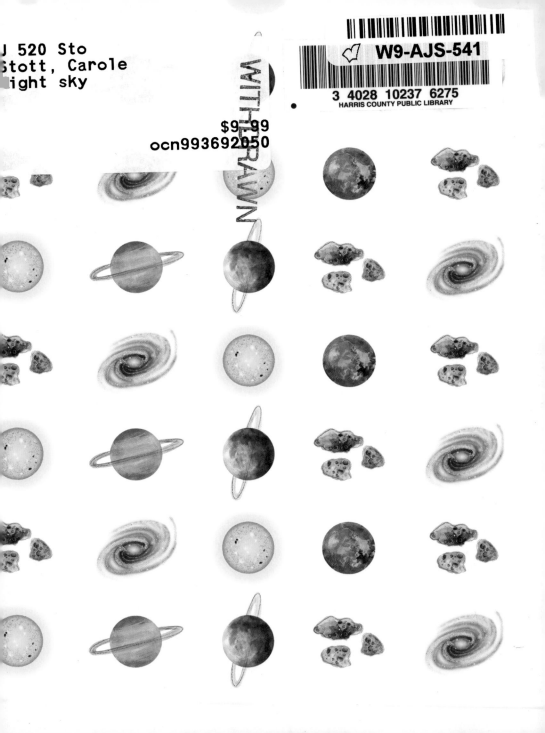

Asteroid belt

The Sun is our
nearest star.

Milky Way

A duststorm
on Mars

Night Sky

Written by Carole Stott

Consultant: Jerry Stone

Penguin Random House

Senior editors Sam Priddy, Jolyon Goddard
US Editor Jill Hamilton
Editor Kritika Gupta
Senior art editor Fiona Macdonald
Project art editor Yamini Panwar
Art editor Roohi Rais
Illustrators Abby Cook, Dan Crisp, Molly Lattin
Jacket coordinator Francesca Young
Jacket designer Rhea Gaughan

DTP designers Ashok Kumar, Dheeraj Singh
Picture researcher Deepak Negi
Producer, pre-production Dragana Puvacic
Producer Isabell Schart
Managing editors Laura Gilbert, Monica Saigal
Managing art editor Diane Peyton Jones
Deputy managing art editor Ivy Sengupta
Art director Martin Wilson
Publishing director Sarah Larter

Original edition
Senior editor Susan McKeever
Editor Bernadette Crowley
Art editor Vicky Wharton
Illustrators Daniel Pyne, Julie Anderson, Nick Hewetson
Production Catherine Semark

The author would like to dedicate this book to Ellen.

First American Edition, 1993
This edition published in the United States in 2018 by DK Publishing
345 Hudson Street, New York, New York 10014

A catalog record for this book
is available from the Library of Congress.
ISBN: 978-1-4654-7339-4

DK books are available at special discounts when purchased in bulk
for sales promotions, premiums, fund-raising, or educational use.
For details, contact: DK Publishing Special Markets, 345 Hudson Street, New York, New York 10014
SpecialSales@dk.com

Printed and bound in China

The publisher would like to thank the following for their kind permission to reproduce their photographs:
(Key: a-above; b-below/bottom; c-center; f-far; l-left; r-right; t-top)
5 Getty Images: Jason Parnell-Brookes / N-Photo Magazine. **7 Dreamstime.com:** PixelParticle. **8 Dreamstime.com:** Ilya Genkin / Igenkin (tr). **10 123RF. com:** solarseven (cl). **Dreamstime.com:** Igor Korionov / Korionov (tr); PixelParticle (cr). **11 123RF.com:** Andrey Alyukhin (tl); Pere Sanz (cr). **NASA:** ESA / Herschel / PACS / MESS Key Programme Supernova Remnant Team; NASA, ESA and Allison Loll / Jeff Hester (Arizona State University) (clb). **13 Dreamstime.com:** Neutronman (cb). **ESO:** Y. Beletsky https://creativecommons.org/licenses/by/4.0 (br). **14 ESO:** GRAVITY consortium/NASA/ESA/M. McCaughrean https://creativecommons.org/licenses/by/4.0 (bl). **15 NASA:** JPL-Caltech (bl). **26 Alamy Stock Photo:** Paul Fearn (tr). **NASA:** JPL-Caltech / Univ. of Toledo (bl). **27 ESO:** INAF-VST/OmegaCAM. Acknowledgement: A. Grado, L. Limatola/INAF-Capodimonte Observatory https://creativecommons. org/licenses/by/4.0 (crb); VISTA/J. Emerson. Acknowledgement: Cambridge Astronomical Survey Unit https://creativecommons.org/licenses/by/4.0 (bl). **28 ESO:** https://creativecommons.org/licenses/by/4.0 (clb, crb). **NASA:** NASA / GSFC / National Center for Supercomputing / Advanced Visualization Laboratoy / B. O'Shea and M. Norman (tr). **29 ESO:** https://creativecommons.org/licenses/by/4.0 (ca, crb); IDA/Danish 1.5 m/R. Gendler, J-E. Ovaldsen, C. Thöne, and C. Feron https://creativecommons.org/licenses/by/4.0 (clb). **Getty Images:** DEA / G. Dagli Orti (tr). **NASA:** JPL / California Institute of Technology (cla). **31 Dreamstime.com:** Zhasmina Ivanova / Zhasminaivanova (crb). **ESO:** Y. Beletsky https://creativecommons.org/licenses/by/4.0 (tr). **36 ESO:** Y. Beletsky https://creativecommons.org/licenses/by/4.0 (ca, crb); Koolander. **38 NASA:** (br). **39 123RF.com:** Atiketta Sangasaeng (tr). **41 Getty Images:** Jason Parnell-Brookes / N-Photo Magazine (tl). **42-43 Dreamstime.com:** Kenneth Keifer / Keifer. **42 NASA:** (bc). **43 NASA:** (tl). **45 NASA:** JPL (tr). **NASA:** JPL / DLR (cr). **47 Dreamstime.com:** Patrimonio Designs Limited / Patrimonio (Moons). **50 NASA:** JPL-Caltech (bl). **51 NASA:** (clb). **53 Dreamstime.com:** Patrimonio Designs Limited / Patrimonio (fcl). **NASA:** JPL / DLR (cl). **55 123RF.com:** qq47182080 (tr). **iStockphoto.com:** StephanHoerold (bl). **56 Getty Images:** John Davis / Stocktrek Images. **57 NASA:** (br); CXC / SAO / M. Karovska et al. (tr). **58 NASA:** GSFC / Elizabeth Zubritsky (tr). **59 123RF.com:** Iurii Kovalenko (br). **NASA:** (clb)

Cover images: **Front: Dreamstime.com:** Ilya Genkin / Igenkin cr; **NASA:** JPL / DLR crb; **Back: Dorling Kindersley:** Andy Crawford tc; **NASA:** tl;
Spine: Dorling Kindersley: Andy Crawford cb

All other images © Dorling Kindersley
For further information see: www.dkimages.com

A WORLD OF IDEAS:
SEE ALL THERE IS TO KNOW

www.dk.com

Contents

Looking at the night sky

Wherever you live in the world, you can look up at the night sky and see the Moon and the twinkling stars. How many stars you see depends on the weather and where you are looking from.

Notebook
Make notes and paint or draw what you see in the sky. Keep a record of the date, the time, and your location.

Starry night
It is best to look at the night sky outside, away from street and house lights, which can block out starlight. You will see the most stars from the countryside, where the sky is darkest. However, if you live in a city, you may still see plenty of stars.

Don't go out alone at night—always ask an adult to go with you.

SEEING STARS

Once outside, you will need a flashlight to see your notebook. Cover your flashlight with red cellophane. A red light will not spoil your eyesight once it is used to the dark. You will need adhesive tape, scissors, and red cellophane.

⚠️ Be careful when using scissors. Always ask an adult to help.

1. Using scissors, cut a piece of red cellophane large enough to cover the end and a little of the side of the flashlight.

2. Stick the cellophane to the flashlight with the adhesive tape, or use a rubber band.

You can gaze at the stars through your bedroom window. Make sure you turn out the lights first or you won't be able to see the stars!

It can be very cold at night, so bundle up well. Remember to bring something to sit on, as well as something to eat and drink.

What's in the night sky?

There is more than you might think in the night sky. You may recognize the Moon and stars, but would you know a planet, a galaxy, or a star "nursery" if you saw one? We can see planets, distant galaxies, and much, much more. It is just a matter of knowing what they look like and where to find them.

The Moon does not always look the same. At times, we see only part of it.

Most of the objects in the night sky are stars.

Comets visit the Earth's sky from time to time.

Spaced out

The Moon is the closest object to Earth, so we can see it very clearly. Other objects you see in the night sky are a lot bigger than the Moon, but because they are so much farther away they only look like dots of light to us.

The Sun is our nearest star. It lights up the daytime sky and blots out everything else. The stars, planets, and galaxies are still there—we just can't see them.

Bang!

Everything we know about exists in the Universe. It began about 14 billion years ago with a huge explosion called the Big Bang. The explosion pushed the young Universe apart. Over millions of years, the matter and energy that was produced from the explosion formed the galaxies, the stars, the planets, and eventually the human race.

There are seven other main planets besides Earth. You can see some of them in the night sky—they often look like bright stars.

Some planets have rings around them.

Millions of stars live together in galaxies. They look like hazy patches of light.

A nebula is a cloud of gas and dust. Stars are being born in this nebula.

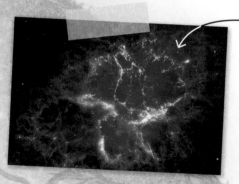

Nebulae are so far away that they too look like hazy patches of light in the sky.

11

What is a star?

There are billions of stars in the Universe. Stars are gigantic balls of glowing gas, which live for millions and millions of years. There are two main gases inside a star—hydrogen and helium. A star uses its gases to produce heat and light. The Sun is a star, and we feel its heat and light on Earth.

In the beginning

Stars are born in spinning clouds made of gas with a little bit of dust mixed in. A force called gravity pulls the gas and dust together, forming vast clouds. The spinning clouds then shrink and form ball shapes.

Star turns

These spinning balls of gas and dust are stars at the start of their lives. If a ball spins slowly it will produce one star. If it spins fast, twin stars are born. Medium spin will produce a star with planets—this is what happened when the Sun was born.

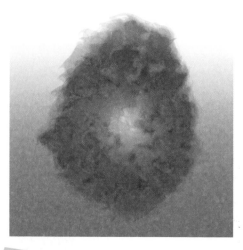

Stars are beginning to form.

Pull and push

Everything in the Universe has its own gravity. Gravity is a pulling force that attracts objects toward one another. Inside a star, gravity battles with a pushing force called pressure. As gravity pulls the gas in, pressure pushes it out, so the gas in a star keeps its ball shape.

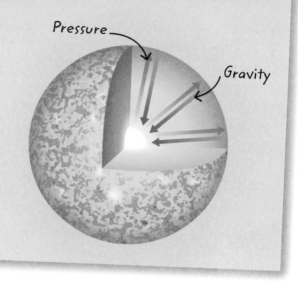

Pressure

Gravity

Young shiners

The young stars start to turn their gases into heat and light and slowly begin to move apart.

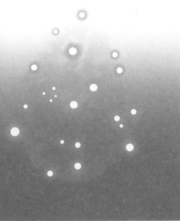

Sisterly stars

The Pleiades (ply-ay-dees) are a group of around 300 very young stars. They are also known as the Seven Sisters because seven of their stars are visible to the naked eye.

Sparklers

A group of stars called the Jewel Box has many colorful stars. You would need a powerful telescope to get this view (right). It looks hazy to the naked eye.

Life of a star

Stars live for millions of years. As a star grows older, it changes. The Universe contains young, middle-aged, and old stars. The biggest stars are more than 1,700 times wider than the Sun, and the smallest stars are much smaller than Earth.

Star colors

All stars are incredibly hot, but some are hotter than others. Blue-white stars are the hottest of all. Yellow-orange ones, like the Sun, are cooler. Red stars are the coolest of all. However, even red stars are more than 13 times hotter than a kitchen oven.

This star is middle-aged, like our Sun. However, its yellow-white color tells us it is hotter and brighter.

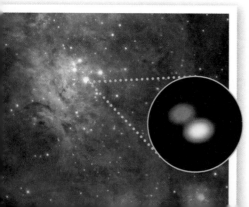

Seeing double

About 80 percent of the stars in the Universe are double stars. These are two stars that live together, or two stars that look close together because we are looking at them from such a long way away. Use binoculars to look for double stars.

Red giant

Different stars change in different ways. How a star changes depends on how much gas it is made of. When stars like the Sun have used up all their hydrogen, their surface will cool and turn red. They will swell up and become red giants. Don't worry though, this won't happen to the Sun for another five billion years!

White dwarf

White dwarf

The red giant Sun will eventually use up all of its fuel. Then it will shrink and become a white dwarf. All the material will pack so close together that the dying Sun will be smaller than Earth.

Supernova

Some stars more massive than the Sun end their lives by blowing themselves apart. When a star explodes like this, it is called a supernova.

The material pushed away in the explosion will produce new stars.

Beware of the black hole!

As some stars die, their material gets more and more squashed together. The stars shrink until they become a point in space. This is called a black hole. Its gravity is so strong that anything that gets too close is sucked into it and can never escape.

15

Dots of light

As we look into space, we see lots of twinkling dots of light. These are huge stars, but because they are so far away they just look like bright specks in a dark sky. It seems as if the Earth is inside a gigantic sphere covered in stars.

The dividing line

The equator, an imaginary line around the middle of Earth, divides our world in two. The top half is the Northern Hemisphere and the bottom half is the Southern Hemisphere. The sphere of stars also has an equator dividing it into two halves. You can see mainly northern stars from the Northern Hemisphere and southern stars from the Southern Hemisphere.

If you live near the equator, you can see stars from both halves of the star sphere.

Northern stars

Star sphere equator

Southern stars

Traveling light

Light travels faster than anything else, but stars are so far away from us that their light takes years to reach Earth. Scientists who study the stars and planets can see distant galaxies whose light started traveling toward us when dinosaurs lived on Earth.

This latitude line is 60° North (of the equator).

60°

30°

The equator is 0° latitude.

0°

This latitude line is 30° South (of the equator)

30°

60°

Which line are you on?

Imaginary lines called latitude lines help us describe where a place is on the Earth's surface. They are counted north or south of the equator and are measured in degrees (°). Knowing which latitude line you live on will help you know which stars are in the sky above your home.

FINDING DIRECTIONS

To study the stars, you'll need to know which direction to look. Make a compass with a stick and some stones.

1. Push the stick into the ground. As the Sun shines on the stick, it will make a shadow. Place your stones at the end of the shadow at different times during the day—the first one in the morning and the last one in the afternoon.

2. The stones will make a curve. The north-south line is where the Sun made the shortest shadow. The east-west line cuts at right angles to it.

The shortest shadow points north if you live in the Northern Hemisphere and south if you live in the Southern Hemisphere.

The four main compass points

North
West — East
South

The north-south line.

Patterns in the sky

When humans first looked at the sky, they saw hundreds of twinkling dots of light. They joined up the dots to make pictures of people, animals, and other things. The pictures helped them, and now us, to remember the stars.

In Greek mythology, Orion was a giant who carried an unbreakable club.

Orion

A group of stars and its picture are called a constellation. This is the constellation of Orion, the hunter. It is one of the easiest constellations to see in the sky.

This fuzzy patch of light in Orion's sword is the Orion Nebula.

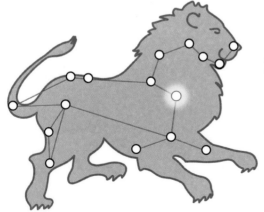

A bright heart

The Lion is another constellation. The Lion's heart is marked by the bright star Regulus. A lion cub cuddles close to the Lion, but its stars are not as bright and it is difficult to see.

MAKE A MODEL OF ORION

The stars in a constellation are different distances away from us. If we could see Orion from somewhere else in space, it would have a different pattern. Make a model of Orion using a shoebox, 19 straws, modeling clay, and the picture of Orion on p. 18.

⚠ Be careful when using scissors. Always ask an adult to help.

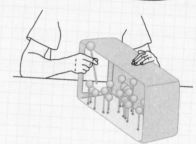

1. Measure the straws from Orion's lower foot to the two stars on Orion's shoulders, one on his head, three on his belt, one on his thigh, and one on his ankle. In the same way, measure straws for the five stars on Orion's right arm and club, and six on the lion's head. Cut one straw for each star. Mold small balls of modeling clay to make the stars and stick one to the end of each straw.

2. Cut a window in one end of the shoebox. Turn the box on its side. Arrange the stars inside the box so that when you look through the window the stars show the pattern of Orion. (Stand the straws in small pieces of modeling clay.)

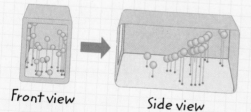

Front view   Side view

3. You can see Orion's pattern through the front window, but from the side you can see how your stars make a completely different pattern. This is how Orion might look from somewhere else in the Milky Way.

Northern stars

If you live in the Northern Hemisphere, look for the constellations on this map. You cannot see all of them in one night. The stars toward the edge of the map can be seen only at certain times of the year. Those in the center are always visible.

Northern sky map

To use this map, turn it so that the current month is at the bottom. The stars in the middle and on the lower half of the map are the stars you can see in that month.

The most visible part of the Great Bear is the seven stars in the shape of a dipper.

The bears up there

There are two bears in the sky—the Great Bear and the Little Bear. These two constellations can be seen all year round. Cepheus (see-fee-us), Cassiopeia (cass-ee-o-pee-uh), and the Dragon can also be seen throughout the year.

The milky river of starlight that stretches across the sky is called the Milky Way.

March

February

January

December

November

Little Dog

Great Dog

Twins

Orion

Bull

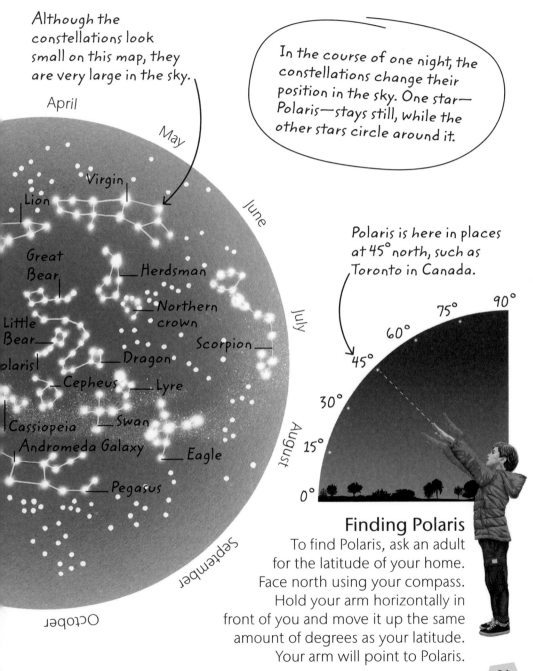

Although the constellations look small on this map, they are very large in the sky.

In the course of one night, the constellations change their position in the sky. One star—Polaris—stays still, while the other stars circle around it.

April

May

June

July

August

September

October

Virgin

Lion

Great Bear

Herdsman

Northern crown

Little Bear

Scorpion

Polaris

Dragon

Cepheus

Lyre

Cassiopeia

Swan

Andromeda Galaxy

Eagle

Pegasus

Polaris is here in places at 45° north, such as Toronto in Canada.

90°

75°

60°

45°

30°

15°

0°

Finding Polaris

To find Polaris, ask an adult for the latitude of your home. Face north using your compass. Hold your arm horizontally in front of you and move it up the same amount of degrees as your latitude. Your arm will point to Polaris.

21

Southern stars

The southern sky is packed with all sizes of constellations. The smallest of all is the Cross. It is visible all year round, just like the other constellations in the center of the map. The constellations at the edge of the map come and go with the seasons.

November

December

January

The Milky Way is very bright in the southern sky.

Orion

River Small Magellan Cloud

Large Magellanic Cloud

Great Dog

Keel

Sail

How to use this map

Turn the map so that the current month is at the bottom. The constellations in the middle and on the lower half of the map are the ones you will be able to see in that month.

February

Little Dog

Lion

Cross

Centaur

Southern Triangle

The constellations around the edge of the map can be seen in both hemispheres.

March

Virgin

April

Can you find which constellations are also on the northern sky map?

May

22

The Cross is made up of four stars. It is small but very bright and easy to spot.

Sirius

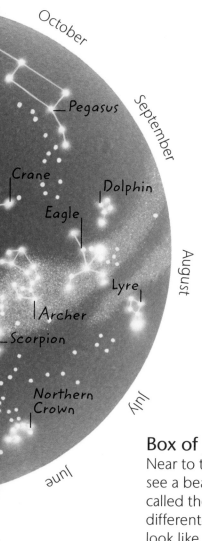

October

Pegasus

September

Crane

Dolphin

Eagle

August

Lyre

Archer

Scorpion

Northern Crown

July

June

Follow that star!

In the spring, face south using your compass and find the Cross. Then swing to the west, and you'll see Sirius, the brightest star in the night sky. Turn to face east and you'll spot Antares, the bright star in the Scorpion.

Nice for a centaur

The Centaur towers over the Cross. In Greek mythology, centaurs were violent creatures who were half-man, half-horse. The Centaur in the sky, named Chiron, was not like other centaurs. He taught hunting, medicine, and music.

In the Centaur is the brightest cluster of old stars— Omega Centauri.

Jewel Box

Box of jewels

Near to the Cross you will see a beautiful group of stars called the Jewel Box. It contains different-colored stars, which look like jewels in the sky.

Cross

The zodiac

The zodiac is a circle of twelve special constellations. The first people on Earth saw that as the Sun, the Moon, and the planets moved through the sky, their paths always crossed the same starry background. They divided this background into twelve constellations, which we now call the zodiac.

The zodiac appears in both hemispheres.

The Sun moves from one zodiac constellation to another every four weeks or so.

Twins Bull Ram Fish Water carrier Sea goat

Crab Lion Virgin Scales Scorpion Archer

Animal circle
The word zodiac comes from the Greek word for animal. Eleven of the zodiac constellations are animals of sorts (humans are animals, too). The constellation of the Scales was named long after the others.

Whenever you look for the Moon and the planets, you'll find them in the circle of zodiac constellations.

The Scorpion

A scorpion is a small but dangerous creature. In Greek mythology, this scorpion stung Orion to death.

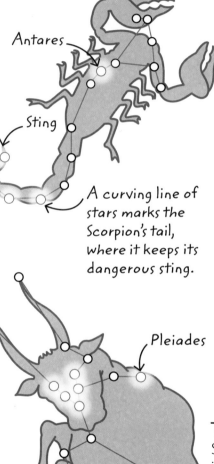

Antares

Sting

A curving line of stars marks the Scorpion's tail, where it keeps its dangerous sting.

Pleiades

STAR PATTERNS

Choose a constellation, such as the Scorpion, to make your own shining star pattern. You will need a piece of cardboard, a pin, a pen or pencil, and a lamp.

⚠ Take care when using drawing pins.

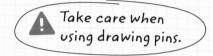

Draw a zodiac pattern on a piece of cardboard. Use a pin to make a hole where each star is.

Shine a light behind the card and see the stars shine.

The Bull

Some star patterns can easily be turned into a picture. In the constellation of the Bull, a V-shape of stars forms his face and then stretches out to make his horns.

Fuzzy objects

In the night sky, stars look like twinkling points of light and planets look like small bright disks. However, you can also see lots of fuzzy dots and patches of misty light in the sky. These may be galaxies that look misty because they are so far away, or they could be clusters of stars or nebulae that are much closer.

Lookalikes
Over 200 years ago, French astronomer Charles Messier started listing fuzzy objects in the sky. Some have names that describe the way they look.

Taking a closer look
Some fuzzy objects we see are not really fuzzy. Clusters of young stars like the Pleiades look fuzzy to your eyes, but you can see they are a group of stars if you use binoculars. Some objects stay fuzzy even when viewed through very powerful telescopes. These objects are nebulae. The word nebula means "misty." Look at the sword in the constellation of Orion and you'll see a misty patch (see p.18).

The Orion Nebula is a huge cloud of gas and dust where stars are born. It is lit up by the young stars in it.

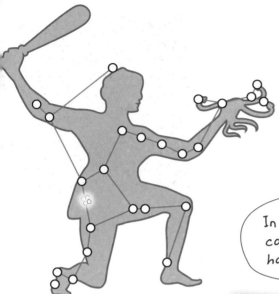

Huge balls of stars

Globular clusters are ball-shaped groups of old stars. They contain hundreds of thousands of stars and look like hazy patches of light in our sky. You can find Hercules between the constellations of the Lyre and the Northern Crown.

In the northern sky, the constellation of Hercules has a bright globular cluster.

Brilliant bunch

The brightest globular cluster in the sky is in the constellation of the Centaur in the southern sky (see p.23). It looks like a hazy patch of light. However, you can see some of its stars with binoculars.

Planetary nebulae

Fuzzy objects such as the Ring Nebula are called planetary nebulae, but they have nothing to do with planets. They are shells of gas blown off by old and dying giant stars.

27

Galaxies

Stars exist together in gigantic groups called galaxies that spin and travel through space. Each galaxy holds many billions of stars, and there are billions of galaxies in the Universe. Between galaxies, there is empty space. There are four different galaxy shapes: spiral, elliptical, barred spiral, and irregular.

Birth of a galaxy

A galaxy starts its life as an enormous spinning cloud of gas and dust. The bigger the cloud, the bigger the galaxy. As the cloud spins, it starts to change shape and stars begin to form.

Starry arm

Central bulge

Spirals

Spiral galaxies are in the shape of flat disks. The stars form arms that spiral out from a big bulge of stars in the center. All types of stars and nebulae can be found in spiral galaxies.

Elliptical

Some galaxies are round like balls. Others are more like squashed balls. Some look as though they have been squashed flat. All of these are elliptical galaxies.

Galaxy gazing

You'll need to look carefully to find a galaxy because it will be very small in the sky. You can see the galaxies shown below, but get your eyes used to the dark first. The star maps on pp.20–23 will show you where to find them.

Magellan

Early astronomers in Europe and Asia could see only the northern sky. Ferdinand Magellan, a Portuguese explorer, sailed south 500 years ago and saw two galaxies. They are now called the Small and Large Magellanic Clouds.

The Andromeda Galaxy is the most distant object you can see without a telescope.

This is the Small Magellanic Cloud in the southern sky.

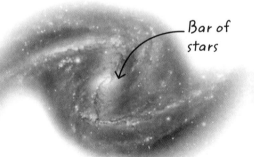

Bar of stars

Barred spirals

In this type of spiral galaxy, the stars form a bar in the center. The arms of stars curl out from both ends of the bar.

Irregulars

Some galaxies have no particular shape at all. These are called irregular galaxies. They are the rarest type of galaxy.

The Milky Way

We live in a galaxy called the Milky Way. It is a spiral galaxy with arms swirling out from its center. There are more stars than you could ever count in our galaxy—around 250 billion. All the stars that you see in the night sky are in the Milky Way.

All types of stars exist in the Milky Way— young, old, big, and small.

Milky Way

If we could fly above the Milky Way, we would see its spiral shape. However, our galaxy is so large that it would take thousands of years to travel to its edge— even in the fastest rocket.

There is a lot of movement in the Milky Way. The stars travel around the galaxy's center, and the whole galaxy spins in space.

Just one of the stars

Although the Sun is special to us, it is just another star in the galaxy. The Sun lies in one of the spiral arms, about one-third of the way out from the galaxy's center.

Milky Way—southern sky

Wherever you live in the world, you can see the path of the Milky Way. It is most spectacular in the sky above the southern half of Earth. Here, you can look to the galaxy's center.

The ancient Greeks thought that the Milky Way was milk spilled by baby Heracles (Hercules) as Hera, the queen of the heavens, fed him her milk.

Side view of the Milky Way

Side view

From out in space, the Milky Way looks like a huge pancake. A side view shows the bulge at its center, where most of the stars live. From Earth, you see a band full of stars stretching across the night sky.

Milky Way—northern sky

You can see the path of the Milky Way with the naked eye. However, using binoculars will show you that the milky light is made of thousands and thousands of stars.

The Sun and its family

The star we know best is the Sun. Like all other stars in the sky, the Sun is an enormous ball of hot, glowing gas. It has its own "family" of planets, including our home—the Earth!

Spots often appear on the Sun's face. They are areas of cooler, dark gas.

Close for comfort

We are nearly 93 million miles (150 million km) away from the Sun—that's close enough for us to learn a lot about it. If we were much closer, we would be roasted alive. The Sun is the only star we can see in detail. Astronomers use special equipment to study it. By learning about the Sun, we learn more about the other stars in the Universe.

Gigantic clouds of hot gas called prominences leap out from the Sun.

Mercury Venus Earth Mars

Sudden bursts of hot, bright gas are called flares.

Jupiter

SEE THE SUN

You must NEVER look directly at the Sun—
its bright light can blind you! However, there is
a safe way to see the Sun. You will need a pair of
binoculars, white paper, thin cardboard, and tape.

⚠️ Take care when you use scissors.

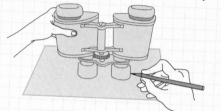

The dark spots
on the image are
sunspots. Draw
over the spots
daily and keep
a record of their
movements.

1. Place the binocular
eyepieces on the cardboard
and draw around them. Cut
out the two circles and push
the eyepieces through the
holes. Tape to hold in place.
Cover one of the big ends of
the binoculars with a lens cap.

2. Position the binoculars so that
sunlight shines through one lens,
as shown. Move the white paper
until you see an image of the
Sun on it.

Far-flung family

The Sun and its family of planets were born from the
same cloud of gas and dust. However, they are so far
apart that it would take the fastest passenger plane
about 650 years to visit the distant dwarf planet Pluto.

Uranus

Neptune

Pluto

Saturn

The Solar System

The Sun and its family are called the Solar System. As
well as the planets, there are more than 170 moons,
millions of small rocks called asteroids, and billions of
comets in the family. The Sun is in the center of the
Solar System—everything else travels around it.

Going around the Sun

Each planet follows its own path,
called an orbit, around the Sun.
All the planets travel in the same
direction, but at different speeds
from each other.

A planet's year is the time it takes
to orbit the Sun once. Neptune's year
is very long—it lasts for about 165
Earth years.

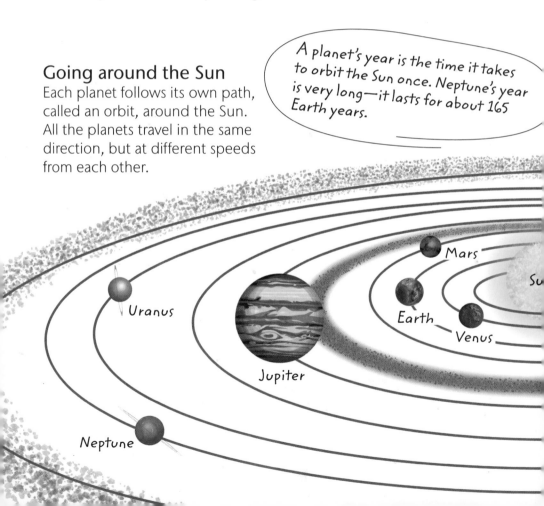

Mars

Uranus

Earth

Venus

Jupiter

Su

Neptune

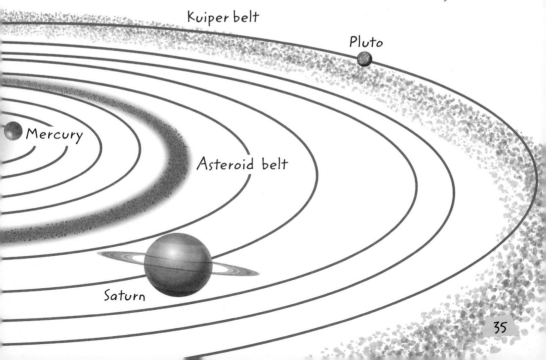

The dwarf planet Ceres is found in the asteroid belt. Four other dwarf planets live in the Kuiper belt.

Big and small

There is a big difference in size between the planets. Mercury is the smallest and Jupiter is the largest. There are also five dwarf planets, including Pluto.

Far from the Sun

Neptune is the farthest main planet from the Sun. However, the dwarf planet Eris is more than twice as far away!

Kuiper belt

Pluto

Mercury

Asteroid belt

Saturn

Mercury and Venus

The two closest planets to the Sun, Mercury and Venus, are both rocky planets, but visitors would find them very different from each other. Mercury is an almost airless world with no atmosphere, or layer of gas around it. Venus is surrounded by a very thick layer of clouds.

Venus's clouds prevent us from seeing its rocky surface.

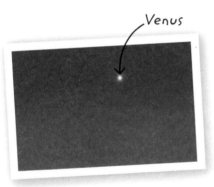
Venus

Bright planet
Venus shines brightly because the clouds that surround it reflect sunlight well. Venus often looks like a very bright star in Earth's sky just before sunrise and just after sunset. Because of this, it is known as the morning or evening star.

Not for humans
Venus is not a friendly place for humans to visit. If you stepped onto its surface, the hot temperature would bake you, the acid in the clouds would poison you, and the high pressure of the atmosphere would crush you.

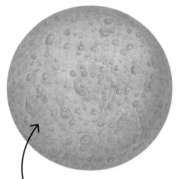

Battered planet

Mercury is covered with bowl-shaped hollows called craters. Mercury's craters were formed millions of years ago when asteroids crashed into it. It is not easy to spot Mercury in the sky because it stays close to the Sun. You may sometimes see it near the horizon—where the Earth meets the sky—at sunrise or sunset.

Without wind or water, Mercury's craters will never wear away.

MAKING CRATERS

Try making your own crater landscape. You will need a washing-up bowl, flour, and objects of different shapes and sizes, such as a ball, a marble, or a stone. These objects will be your "asteroids."

1. Pour some flour into a bowl, spread it out evenly, and smooth down the surface with a spoon. The flour should be about 2 inches (5 cm) deep. This will be your "landscape."

2. Place the bowl on some newspaper on the floor. Drop your asteroids onto your landscape.

It might be best to do this outside!

3. See how different-sized asteroids make different-sized craters. Bigger asteroids make wider and deeper craters. Try throwing the asteroids at different speeds. The faster they travel, the more impact they have on the landscape.

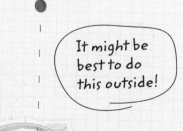

Planet Earth

There is no other planet like Earth. As far as we know, it is the only planet where there is life. Earth hasn't always looked like it does today, nor will it stay the same. Volcanoes, earthquakes, the weather, and humans all change the Earth in different ways.

The Earth is made mostly of rock and metal.

Journey to Earth

Imagine traveling to Earth from far away in space. At first, it would look like a blue planet. However, as you got closer, you would see white clouds, then brown and green land and oceans of water.

Water covers three-quarters of the Earth's surface.

Earthshine

If you were on the Moon, the Earth would shine but would not move across the sky. The part of Earth you see here is in daylight. It is night for the other, dark side.

The Earth is like a spaceship traveling through space. As it orbits the Sun, it is moving more than 100 times faster than a jumbo jet!

Bright lights glow across the sky.

Light fantastic
The Sun blasts out particles, or tiny pieces, which enter Earth's atmosphere and create amazing light displays. These displays can be seen in the sky toward the North and South Poles. They are known as the northern and the southern lights.

Earth is made up of several layers.

Story of the Earth
Earth is about 4.5 billion years old. In the beginning, it was so hot that most of its metals and rocks melted. Over time, the outer layer cooled to form a solid crust and the metals sank to the Earth's center. As the Earth cooled, steam fell as rain and formed the oceans.

The changing Moon

The Moon orbits the Earth as the Earth orbits the Sun. We can see the Moon most nights and often during the day, too. However, the Moon we see seems to change shape in a 29.5-day cycle. The different shapes of the Moon we see are called its phases.

Moon views

As the Moon orbits the Earth, our view of it changes as the Sun lights up more or less of the side we see. At times, it seems to disappear altogether.

Last quarter—it is on the last quarter of its orbit.

Crescent—it will soon disappear again.

New Moon— we cannot see it because none of the side that faces us is lit up.

The Sun lights up the Moon and the Earth.

Crescent— the Sun begins to light up our side of the Moon.

First quarter—it has moved around the first quarter of its orbit.

40

Moon moves

Everything in the sky moves. The Moon follows a path across the sky, and if you look at it from time to time one evening, you'll see how its position changes. In this view (left), less than one hour has passed between the top and bottom Moons.

Gibbous—when the Moon gets "smaller," it is said to be waning.

Full Moon—all of the side facing us is lit up.

Gibbous—three-quarters is visible. The "growing" Moon is said to be waxing.

The Moon in close-up

You can see surface details on the Moon—even in the daytime—and you do not need any special equipment. There are no clouds on the Moon to spoil your view. The dark patches you see are lowlands while the brighter areas are highlands.

Moon watch

As long as the weather is fine, you will be able to see the Moon regularly and record its changing phases. You can also make drawings of its landscape. Once you have studied the Moon with your eyes, look at it through binoculars to see even more detail.

Moon walkers

The Earth and the Moon are the only places where humans have walked. So far, 24 people have been to the Moon and 12 have walked on its surface. The next time astronauts visit the Moon, they may set up a base camp where visitors can stay.

We always see the same side of the Moon—this side.

High jumps

Everyday life on the Moon would be very different from life on Earth. There would be no noise because sound cannot travel without air. Also, the Moon's gravity is much weaker, so you could jump almost six times higher than on Earth.

A MOON OF YOUR OWN

Make a model of the Moon. You will need newspaper, one cup flour, three cups water, a ball, plastic wrap, string, tape, and paint.

1. Mix the flour with water. Soak some newspaper pieces in the mixture. Cover the ball with plastic wrap and plaster half of the ball with four layers of the wet paper. When it has dried, remove the half-Moon from the ball and make another.

2. Attach one end of the string to the inside of one half-Moon. Put the two halves together and secure with tape. Cover the join with three layers of wet newspaper.

3. When dry, use the pictures in this book to help you paint your Moon. You can make craters and highlands with more wet paper. Use the string to hang it up.

The Moon's craters, like Mercury's, were made by space rocks crashing into it thousands of millions of years ago.

Mars

One hundred years ago, some scientists believed that intelligent life lived on Mars. However, we do not have proof of that.

If you were going to choose a planet to visit, Mars would be the best place to go. It is the next planet from the Sun after the Earth, so it is not too far away. Its surface is the most like the Earth's, although it is very cold on Mars. There is no air to keep animals and plants alive, red rocks and dust are everywhere, and even the sky is red.

Dust and rust

Why is Mars called the red planet? Because from the Earth, it looks like a red disk! Spacecraft that landed on Mars found that the red color comes from rusty iron dust.

Violent volcano

Mars has giant volcanoes on its surface. Long ago, they erupted and helped change the surface of Mars—but today they are all dead. The biggest volcano is Olympus Mons. It is three times bigger than the highest mountain on Earth.

Olympus Mons

The red dust covers everything on the planet.

The Martian air is always freezing cold.

Viking photo

This photograph of Mars's barren, rocky surface was taken by the American spacecraft *Viking 2*. Scientists are now planning to send an astronaut to Mars. He or she should be on Mars when you are an adult. Perhaps you will become an astronaut, and it could be you!

Storms of dust

Mars has duststorms that can last for weeks. Strong winds pick up the red dust and move it about the surface. With powerful telescopes, we can see the change in the color of Mars as the dust moves around.

Swirling red dust

Mars has ice caps on its north and south poles.

Jupiter

Gigantic Jupiter is made mostly of gas and liquid, with a small rocky core, or center. Jupiter has a cloudy outer layer with dark bands and bright zones of different colors. The cloud tops reflect sunlight well, so the planet shines brightly in our sky.

Jupiter's cloud layer is icy cold. However, the planet gets hotter and hotter toward the center.

Jupiter's journey

Jupiter can be mistaken for a bright silver-white star in the night sky. It moves slowly against the starry background, and you can watch its progress from week to week. It takes about a year to travel through each zodiac constellation.

Europa

Stormy weather

Jupiter spins around very fast. This produces high-speed winds and terrific storms. These are much bigger and longer-lasting than storms on Earth. The Great Red Spot storm has been raging for at least 300 years!

The Great Red Spot is the biggest storm in the Solar System.

Cross section

Jupiter's layer of clouds is made mostly of hydrogen gas. Underneath the layer of clouds is a sea of liquid hydrogen. Beneath it is more hydrogen, in the form of metal. At the center is the planet's rocky metal core.

The cloud layer is 800 miles (1,280 km) thick.

Rocky metal core

Metal hydrogen

Sea of liquid hydrogen

Many moons

In 2017, the 69th moon of Jupiter was discovered. The four biggest— Ganymede, Callisto, Io, and Europa— can be seen from Earth with binoculars.

Callisto

Ganymede

Jupiter has a faint ring that was discovered by a spacecraft in 1979. The ring cannot be seen from Earth, even through the most powerful telescopes.

Io

Earth meal

The Earth is tiny compared to Jupiter. It would take 1,321 Earth-sized mouthfuls to fill up Jupiter.

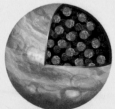

If you would like to visit Jupiter on your next school trip—you're out of luck. Jupiter is so far away it would take a bus almost 1,800 years to get there!

Saturn

Like Jupiter, Saturn is a giant planet made mainly of gas and liquid. It is surrounded by a system of rings that stretches for thousands of miles into space. Saturn has 62 moons.

If Saturn could be placed in water, it would float!

Winds ten times faster than hurricanes on Earth whizz around Saturn.

Colorful clouds
Saturn's clouds are colored by the different materials in them. Scientists have looked through holes in the top layer of gold-colored clouds and seen brown and blue clouds below.

The rings can be seen only through a telescope.

Saturn's rings are not solid. They are made of millions of pieces of rock and ice.

Big ears!
When astronomers first saw Saturn's rings more than 400 years ago, they didn't know what they were. Saturn looked as though it had ears!

View of the rings

Our view of Saturn's rings changes as it orbits the Sun. Every 15 years, Saturn is sideways to us and the rings seem to disappear.

Sometimes we get an excellent view of the rings.

Our sideways view of Saturn

Sometimes we can see the underside of the rings.

Close-up

Some of Saturn's rings are made of small pieces that are like icy dust. Other rings contain big, car-sized boulders.

MAGNETIC PLANETS

Some planets are giant magnets, with a force that stretches into space. Use iron filings, a magnet, thin cardboard, and half a plastic ball to show the magnetic force around a planet.

⚠ Be careful with the iron filings—don't inhale them or get them in your eyes.

1. Place the half-ball on the cardboard. Scatter a fine layer of iron filings over the ball.

2. Carefully lift the cardboard and place it over the magnet. Tap it lightly. The iron filings will form a pattern of lines around the ball.

3. You'll see the lines curve outward. Some planets have lines of magnetic force around them. The lines come from the planets' north and south poles.

Uranus and Neptune

These two "ice giants" are so far away that you need powerful telescopes to see them. We have learned most of what we know about them from the space probe *Voyager 2*. Both planets are made mostly of gas and ice and are very cold.

Uranus's "ring" is made up of 13 separate rings of dark rock.

Side spin

Uranus's outer layers are made mostly of hydrogen and helium gas. Another gas, called methane, gives the planet its blue-green color. Uranus spins on its side as it orbits the Sun. A system of rings and 27 moons orbit around Uranus's middle.

Voyager 2 sent thousands of pictures back to Earth.

Uranus's summer lasts for 42 years! However, summer on Uranus is very cold.

A long journey

Voyager 2 left Earth in 1977 to travel to the distant giants of the Solar System. After visiting Jupiter and Saturn, it reached Uranus in 1986 and Neptune in 1989.

Feeling blue

Neptune is made of the same gases as Uranus. It also gets its rich coloring from the sunlight shining on the methane gas. Neptune's color is more intense because we can see into its atmosphere. We can also see dark and light spots on its surface.

Neptune is the windiest planet in the Solar System.

Neptune's rings are very dim.

White spots are clouds of methane ice.

One white patch on Neptune travels so fast that it has been nicknamed "Scooter."

The Great Dark Spot is a huge storm. It is almost as big as planet Earth.

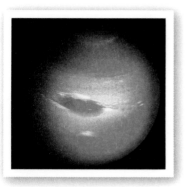

Racing round

Neptune's dark and white spots all travel around the planet at different speeds. Sometimes they are close together, while at other times they are apart.

M V E M   J   S   U   N

Order of the planets

Make up a sentence using the first letter of each of the main planets' names to help you remember their order out from the Sun. Start with "M" for the first planet—Mercury. For example: Many Very Elderly Men Just Snooze Under Newspapers.

Pluto, moons, and asteroids

The dwarf planet Pluto is so small and so distant from Earth that we cannot get a good look at it—even with the most powerful telescopes. Pluto has five moons—the largest is called Charon, which is about half its size. There are about 170 other moons in the Solar System, 69 of them living with Jupiter. Mercury and Venus are the only planets without any moons.

Small world

Pluto is really tiny—much smaller than Earth's Moon. It is a freezing and dark world of ice and rock. The Sun is so far away that Pluto gets hardly any heat and light from it.

Some scientists think Pluto was once a moon of Neptune that got knocked out of its orbit.

From Pluto, the Sun would look like just another bright star.

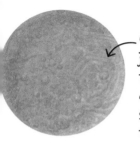

Charon takes just over 6 days to travel once around Pluto—the same time it takes to rotate.

Charon

Pluto was discovered in 1930 and Charon in 1978. Charon is rocky and icy like Pluto. In 2015, the *New Horizons* spacecraft flew past Pluto and Charon.

Ganymede   Europa   Io

Many moons

Moons do not all look the same. Ganymede, one of Jupiter's moons, is icy and covered in craters, Europa is smooth and covered with dark lines, and eruptive Io looks like a giant pizza!

Asteroid belt

There are millions of small rocky bodies called asteroids in the Solar System. Most lie in between Mars and Jupiter and travel around the Sun together. They form an enormous belt around the Sun.

Moons or asteroids?

Mars has two tiny moons, Phobos and Deimos. They are potato shaped, just like some asteroids. It is possible they were once asteroids that were captured by Mars's gravity.

53

Comets and meteors

Comets are enormous balls of snow and dust, like gigantic dirty snowballs. They live together in a huge cloud at the edge of our Solar System. Occasionally, a comet is knocked out of the cloud and starts a journey toward the Sun. You may see one in the night sky as it passes by Earth—it will look like a fuzzy star.

A comet's tail can be millions of miles in length.

The main body of the comet, the nucleus, is in the middle of this big head of gas and dust, called the coma.

Hot and dusty

Some comets travel into the main part of the Solar System. As a comet approaches the Sun, the Sun's heat starts to turn the comet's dirty snow into gas and dust. A tail grows as the comet loses material. The tail gets smaller and smaller as the comet moves away from the Sun.

Halley's return

Some comets can be seen again and again in the night sky. A comet called Halley's Comet orbits the Sun once every 76 years or so. Comets like Halley's don't last forever. They lose material as they travel. If Earth moves through this material, we see a meteor shower in the night sky.

The tail is longest near the Sun.

The tail starts to grow.

The tail always points away from the Sun.

The tail disappears as the comet moves away from the Sun's heat.

A light shower

During a meteor shower, streaks of light cross the night sky as rocky material burns up in our atmosphere. Meteors are also called shooting stars. Look out for the Geminids shower, which occurs around December 7–17 every year. You can see up to 50 shooting stars in an hour.

Arizona crater

Large space rocks that are too big to burn up in the atmosphere crash into Earth's surface. These are called meteorites. The big Barringer meteorite made this 0.7-mile- (1.2-km-) wide crater in Arizona in the United States around 50,000 years ago.

55

Astronomers' tools

Astronomers use special tools to study the stars and planets. The telescope is the most important tool for finding out about the night sky, but astronomers do not look through telescopes very often. Modern telescopes work on their own, using cameras and computers to record what they see. This information is then passed on to the astronomer, who works in an office.

Above the clouds

Telescopes are kept in dome-shaped buildings called observatories. The world's best observatories are placed high on mountain tops. This places the telescopes above the clouds and keeps them away from city lights, which would spoil the view.

The observatory's dome-shaped roof slides open when the telescope is to be used.

Telescopes like this one can take photographs.

Space probes

Earth's atmosphere stops some information from space reaching us. To overcome this problem, astronomers send out machines, called space probes, to get a closer look at the planets. Other spacecraft, called satellites, orbit Earth above the atmosphere and look out into space.

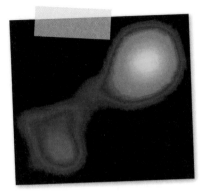

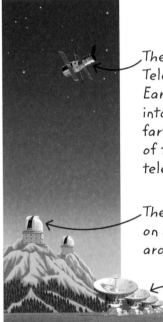

The Hubble Space Telescope orbits Earth. It looks out into space, seeing farther than any of the Earth-based telescopes.

There are observatories on mountain tops all around the world.

Special telescopes, called radio telescopes, listen to the stars.

Seeing into a star

Different tools look at the stars in different ways. X-ray satellites take X-ray pictures. A star may not shine very brightly, but an X-ray picture might show that there is a lot of activity in the star and that it has lots of energy.

A great help

Computers control telescopes, satellites, and space probes, and also help astronomers work out what they have seen. In modern astronomy, computers are just as important as telescopes.

Exploring space

We can learn a lot about what is in space by watching from Earth. However, by traveling into space, we can get a better look and even see things that are invisible from Earth. Astronomers regularly send out satellites and space probes. Astronauts—human space travelers—have also explored space close to Earth.

Getting the message
On Earth, big dishes work like enormous ears, collecting the radio messages sent by space probes.

Galileo
A space probe called *Galileo* was sent on a mission to Jupiter in 1989. It took *Galileo* six years to reach Jupiter, even though space probes travel very fast. Once at Jupiter, *Galileo* spent eight years touring around the giant planet and its moons.

The "umbrella" part was used to communicate with Earth.

Camera

The main part of Galileo was about the size of a bus.

Galileo had a small probe, which it dropped into Jupiter's atmosphere.

Jupiter's magnetic force was measured by this long arm.

LIFT OFF

Rockets carry satellites, space probes, and astronauts into space. Use a balloon to see how a rocket blasts off from Earth.

1. Blow up the balloon but don't tie the end—hold it between your fingers instead.

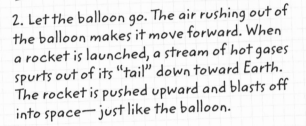

2. Let the balloon go. The air rushing out of the balloon makes it move forward. When a rocket is launched, a stream of hot gases spurts out of its "tail" down toward Earth. The rocket is pushed upward and blasts off into space—just like the balloon.

Catch that drink

Everything is almost weightless in space. Things have to be tied down in case they float away. Drinks are sucked through straws. If any escapes, the drink forms into small balls, which float like little balloons.

A pack on the back

When astronauts are outside their spacecraft they must be careful not to fly off into space. Sometimes they wear backpacks that contain small rockets, allowing the astronauts to control their movements.

Index

Acknowledgments

DK Publishing
would like to thank:

Helen Peters for the index.
David Hughes for checking
the text.

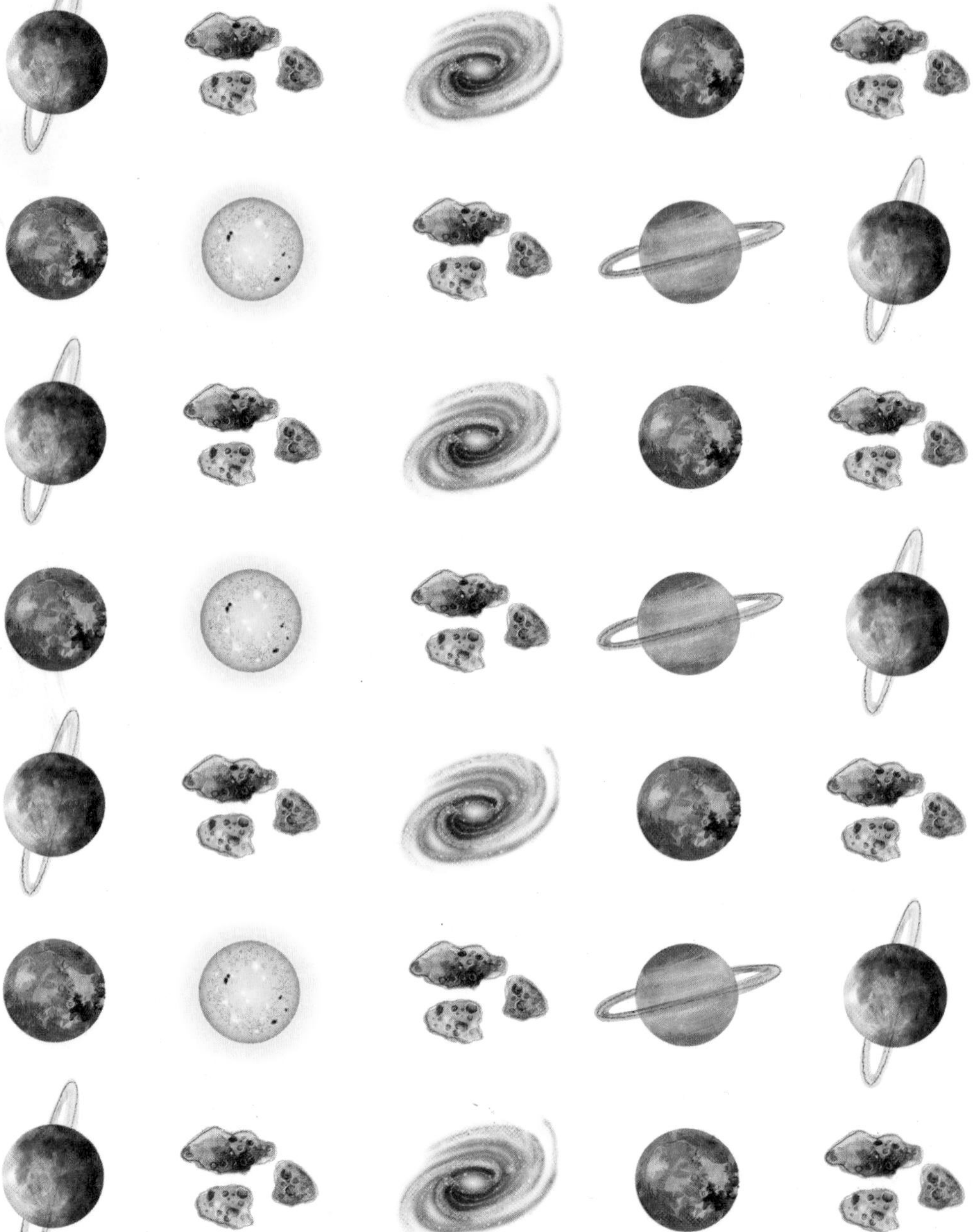